THE WOMAN IN WHITE

Music by
ANDREW LLOYD WEBBER

Lyrics by
DAVID ZIPPEL

ISBN 0-634-06407-X

Original songbook arrangements by David Cullen
Adapted by Justin Pyne

Production photographs by Manuel Harlan
Book designed by Dewynters, London

World Premiere at The Palace Theatre,
London 15th September 2004

www.womaninwhitethemusical.com

HAL•LEONARD®
CORPORATION
7777 W. BLUEMOUND RD. P.O. BOX 13819 MILWAUKEE, WI 53213

Visit Hal Leonard Online at
www.halleonard.com

THE WOMAN

IN WHITE

Contents

TRYING NOT TO NOTICE

Music by ANDREW LLOYD WEBBER
Lyrics by DAVID ZIPPEL

I BELIEVE MY HEART

Music by ANDREW LLOYD WEBBER
Lyrics by DAVID ZIPPEL

HARTRIGHT:

When-ev-er I look at you,___ the world dis-ap-

pears. All in a sin-gle glance so re-veal-ing.___

YOU SEE I AM NO GHOST

Music by ANDREW LLOYD WEBBER
Lyrics by DAVID ZIPPEL

Moderately

You see I am no ghost be-fore you. I am flesh and blood, be-

lieve your eyes. Kind sir, my name is Anne, Anne Cath-'rick, and be-

lieve my words, I tell no lies. Limm-'ridge was my home in child-hood,

ALL FOR LAURA

Music by ANDREW LLOYD WEBBER
Lyrics by DAVID ZIPPEL

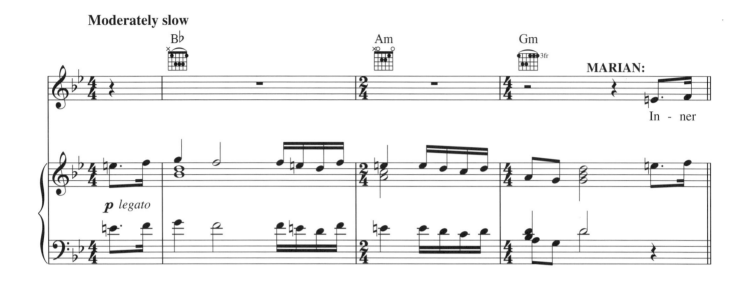

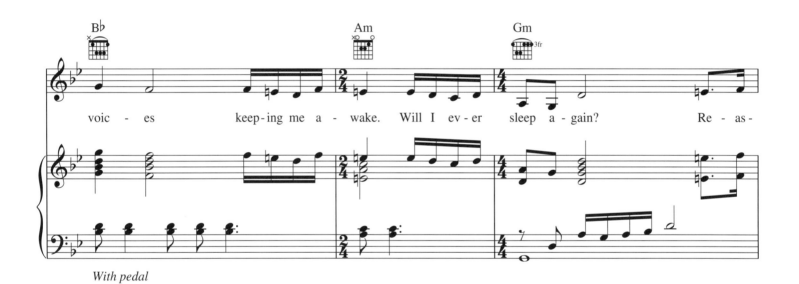

IF I COULD ONLY DREAM
THIS WORLD AWAY

Music by ANDREW LLOYD WEBBER
Lyrics by DAVID ZIPPEL

Moderately

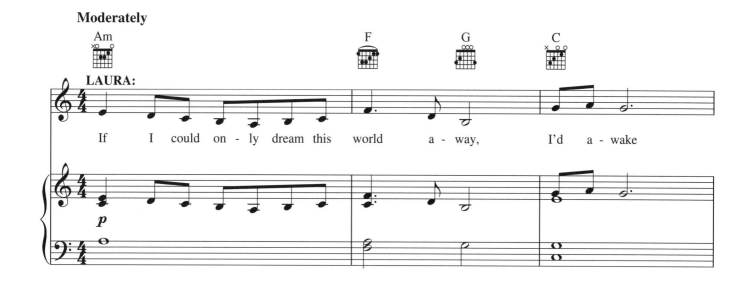

LAURA:
If I could on-ly dream this world a - way, I'd a - wake

in your arms. If I could keep this bit - ter life at bay,

wide a - wake in your arms.___ The vow that keeps me

EVERMORE WITHOUT YOU

Music by ANDREW LLOYD WEBBER
Lyrics by DAVID ZIPPEL

Were we nev-er meant to be?

Nev-er more a-lone, _____ nev-er to for-get you. _____

LOST SOULS

Music by ANDREW LLOYD WEBBER
Lyrics by DAVID ZIPPEL

Repeat and Fade

YOU CAN GET AWAY WITH ANYTHING

Music by ANDREW LLOYD WEBBER
Lyrics by DAVID ZIPPEL

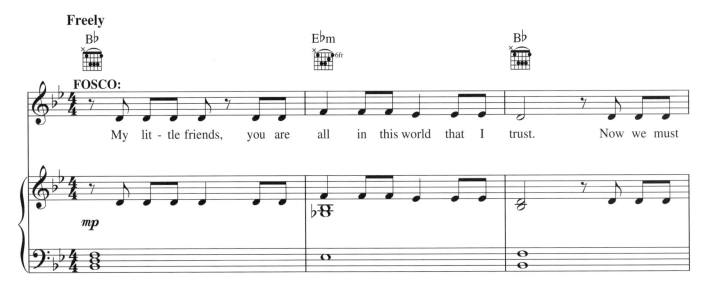

FOSCO: My lit - tle friends, you are all in this world that I trust. Now we must

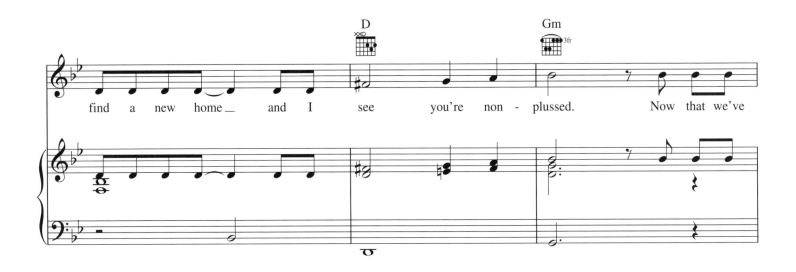

find a new home __ and I see you're non - plussed. Now that we've

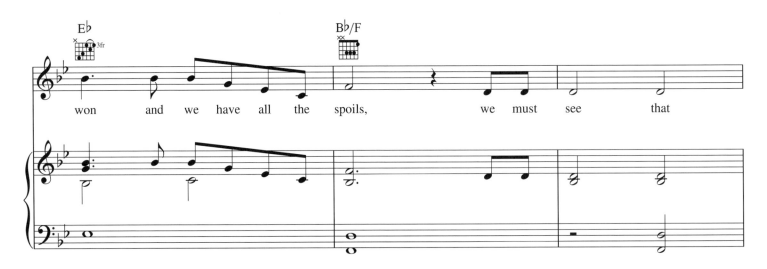

won and we have all the spoils, we must see that

THE SEDUCTION

Music by ANDREW LLOYD WEBBER
Lyrics by DAVID ZIPPEL

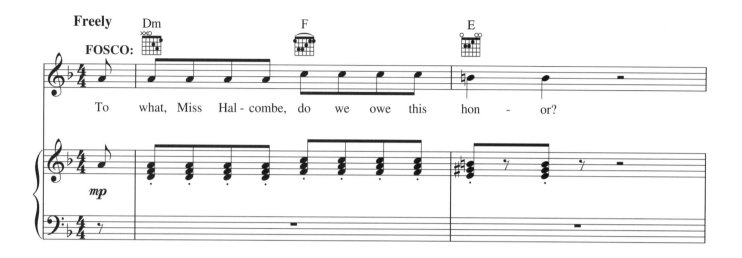

To what, Miss Hal-combe, do we owe this hon-or?

Each suc-ces-sive day was get-ting dull - er. Well, I some-how thought you might be

miss-ing me. I must tell you scar-let is your col - or.

60